A Field Guide
to North American
Birders

A Field Guide to North American Birders

A Parody

MARGARET HARMON

B
BERKLEY BOOKS, NEW YORK

A Berkley Book
Published by The Berkley Publishing Group
A division of Penguin Putnam Inc.
375 Hudson Street
New York, New York 10014

This is a work of fiction. Names, characters, places, and incidents
are either the product of the author's imagination or are used fictitiously,
and any resemblance to actual persons, living or dead, business
establishments, events, or locales is entirely coincidental.

PRINTING HISTORY
Berkley trade paperback edition / April 2001

The Penguin Putnam Inc. World Wide Web site address is
http://www.penguinputnam.com

Library of Congress Cataloging-in-Publication Data

Harmon, Margaret, 1940–
    A field guide to North American birders : a parody / Margaret Harmon ;
[cover and interior art by Margaret Harmon].—Berkley trade pbk. ed.
        p. cm.
    ISBN 0-425-17835-8 (pbk.)
    1. Birds—Humor. 2. Bird watchers—Humor. 3. Bird watching—Humor.
4. Peterson, Roger Tory, 1908——Parodies, imitations, etc. I. Title.

PN6231.B46 H37 2001
818'.5407—dc21   2001016174

PRINTED IN THE UNITED STATES OF AMERICA

10   9   8   7   6   5   4   3   2   1

Contents

Part III: Support for the Serious Birder-watcher

Acknowledgments

The following birders have generously contributed to this field guide: Jean E. Thomson Black, Carol Carkeek, Jim Coatsworth, Mike Fink, Bill Haas, Wayne Harmon, Marjorie Hastings, Tania Ireton, Dave and Gail Kniffing, Kathy Knight, Ken Kurland, Nola Lamken, Ginger and Chuck Laws, Mike and Genevieve Matherly, Guy McCaskie, Bill McCausland, Teri O'Nele, Carol Parker, Jim Peugh, Douglas Pratt, Phil Pryde, Andrew Richford, Geoff Rogers, Bob Shanks, John Sill, Ken Simpson, Jeff Spaulding, Spike Wolfensberger, and Peter Yingling.

I also thank Fritz Harmon, Andrea Matone, Dorothy Ledbetter, Bette Pegas, and Cheryl Staples for key insights and loyal support—and my agent, Jo Fagan; editor, Natalee Rosenstein; and art director, Steve Ferlauto, for being a *delightful* team.

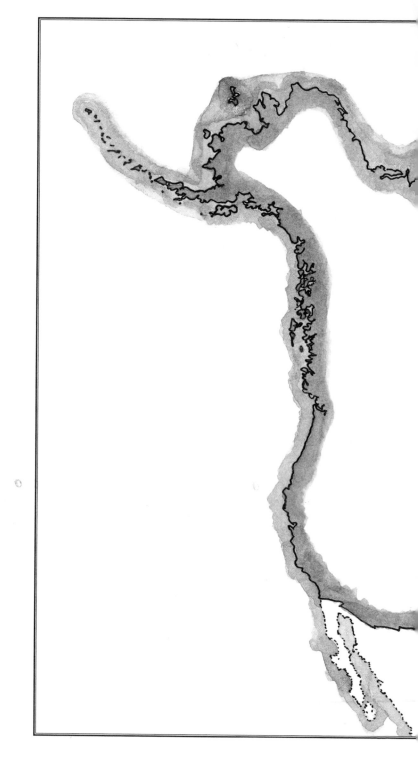

North America

for the

American
Birder-watching
Society

Part 1

Birder-watching

Using This Guide

A Field Guide to North American Birders is a handbook for the serious observer of birders. Species descriptions and patternistic drawings pinpoint field marks, making it possible to identify birders discreetly—certainly without shooting them to measure body parts. Based upon original research into birder behavior, the guide uses only current names supported by DNA and rulings of the American Birder-watching Society.

Let us say here that *observing* is not snooping. It is by *observation* that hominids have found pattern within chaos and come to dominate the planet. The scrutiny of birders fits comfortably within the naturalist tradition. With simple tools— unobtrusive handheld tape recorder, the binoculars that give us entrée to the group, and tiny pen and paper—we can study earth's preeminent species without arousing hostility or fear.

Birder-watching, beyond its fashionability, is a wholesome outdoor social activity drawing us into a closer relationship with the earth, in the company of people who make us feel it's okay to be human. Birder-watchers build fitness, enjoy social outings that needn't be reciprocated, make friends without getting too close, and learn masses of information on which we may privately grade ourselves *A+, Superior, Well Done, Excellent*, while publicly maintaining the trademark birder-watcher modesty.

Human beings, at the top of food and power chains, possess mechanical, if not physical, means to come and go at will. So only keen birder-watchers armed with knowledge of habitat and behavior can enjoy the company of these fascinating creatures. May this guide enhance your enjoyment in the field.

Anatomy of a Birder

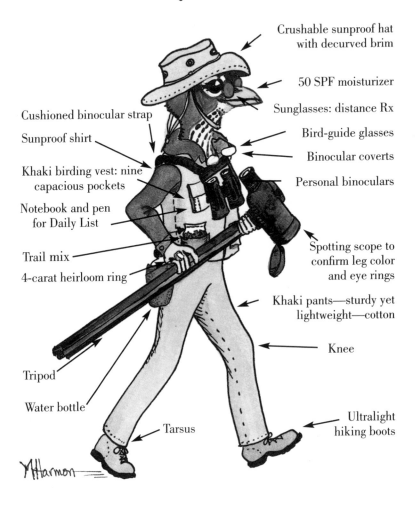

Crushable sunproof hat
with decurved brim

50 SPF moisturizer

Sunglasses: distance Rx

Bird-guide glasses

Binocular coverts

Personal binoculars

Cushioned binocular strap

Sunproof shirt

Khaki birding vest: nine
capacious pockets

Notebook and pen
for Daily List

Trail mix

4-carat heirloom ring

Spotting scope to
confirm leg color
and eye rings

Khaki pants—sturdy yet
lightweight—cotton

Knee

Tripod

Water bottle

Tarsus

Ultralight
hiking boots

MHarmon

Birder Songs and Calls

Birder vocalizations are divided into songs and calls. **Songs,** usually complex, are considered sexual—to establish territory or attract mates. Example:

Yes, I bird this estuary—dawn and dusk.

SUBVOCAL SONGS are common, but difficult to verify. Example:

(Thought or muttered)*: I saw that Yellow-throated Warbler first. When I asked, "What's that bird?" they didn't even lift their binoculars. Then, when she saw it, they all looked right away. I saw it three minutes before anybody else. It's my Yellow-throated Warbler.* Mine, mine, mine.

CALLS are simple, brief bursts of information—descriptions, warnings, expressions of alarm, or attempts to maintain contact—uttered during any season. Examples:

> *STOP!!! An elf owl!!!* (On crowded two-lane road with no shoulder.)

> *Is that you, Sweetheart???* (In areas posted for bears.)

In addition to intraspecies vocalizations, birders make poignant attempts at interspecies communication, in four categories:

- **Pishing** (forcing air between the tongue, teeth, and lips, in imitation of certain birdsongs) can pierce thickets and roust birds a quarter mile away. Pishers persist, whether birds greet or attack them.

- **Kissing** two fingers or the back of one's hand mimics the shrill squeal of a rodent in the talons of a raptor. The intent is to call in those birds who fly by slowly and gawk at roadkill.

- **Transliterating** birdsongs into human speech attracts bilingual birds. Example:

> Birder: *Who cooks for you? Who cooks for you?*
> Bird: *I eat raw food, thanks; who cooks for you?*

- **Tool using**—including tape recorders, mechanical squeakers, and whistles—maximizes human effectiveness. But even when recording actual birdsongs, birders risk avian ridicule:

Birder (playing birdsong tape): *Heyyy, baaaby, I have fifty twigs in a nestbox!*

Bird: *Pffffft!! Mating season was two months ago; we leave for Antarctica at dawn.*

Birder: *Heyyy, baaaby, I have fifty twigs in a nestbox! Heyyy, baaaby, I have fifty twigs in a nestbox! Heyyy, baaaby, I have fifty twigs in a nestbox!*

Mistakes are unquestionably made. But who among us is not charmed by attempts to transcend species barriers?

Stages of a Birder

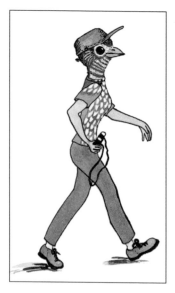

BEGINNING
Garage Sale Binoculars

INTERMEDIATE
The Correct Tool for Every Task

ADVANCED
Optics

Birder Maturation

Birders are semi-altricial: At birth they can open their eyes and cry, but are naked and unable to stand, run, fly, swim far, shelter themselves, or prepare food. Like other humans, birders require long-term parenting.

After achieving adult size and markings, however, birders continue to learn, sometimes lifelong. The Six Developmental Phases of a birder are reflected in their speech at different ages.

1. "YOOK! A bu'ud!"

2. "It's a sparrow."

3. "That's a House Sparrow."

4. "Here's a Lark Sparrow."

5. "There's a male Henslow's Sparrow in the scope."

6. "We're going to California Gulch to get the Five-striped Sparrow."

Attracting Birders to Your Yard

PLAN 1: Buy a house on land adjoining a national park and landscape your yard with native flora. Set out feeders dispensing flower nectar, black sunflower seeds, Niger thistle, suet, orange wedges, stunned insects, tame fish, and dark and milk chocolate truffles. Invite an Audubon chapter to schedule field trips *chez vous*.

PLAN 2: Call several rare bird hotlines to report a female Siberian Rubythroat in your rock garden. Mention that your wildlife photographer spouse got excellent photos of the bird, and prints are being sent for analysis to the Smithsonian, American Ornithologists' Union, Audubon Society, American Birding Association, a prominent natural history museum, and Jon Dunn, Pete Dunne, Kenn Kaufman, Father Tom, and H. Douglas Pratt.

A day later, call to report that the Rubythroat's mate has joined her, confirming the identification.

NOTE: If you do opt for Plan 2, be sure to photograph, record, and enjoy your birders because you'll have to move away, change your name, and dye your hair.

Identifying Birders

Take time to familiarize yourself with the illustrations and descriptions of birders in your guide, arranged in the classic loons to finches order. You will immediately recognize familiar birders—and add new birders to your personal must-see list.

In the field, the key to identifying birders is resisting the temptation to rush to the field guide before observing astutely and, if possible, jotting down your observations. Is your birder male or female? Adult or juvenile? Modestly equipped or professionally geared? Is he sure-voiced or questioning? Is she pishing or scowling at someone who is? Is he engaging in distinctive behavior you've never seen before?

Sketch markings and note eye color. Discreetly tape-record vocalizations. Observe gestures. Ascertain motives. Look for *patterns* of behavior.

Only then consult your field guide. If the birder leaves, you'll still have your field notes. And you won't be confused by descriptions and illustrations of other birders. In this guide, distinguishing characteristics are mentioned in the text, and striking physical features are illustrated.

Patience and precision are essential, but joy is our compass. We each have our own favorite birders.

One does feel triumphant, though, calling out common and scientific names faster than field psychologists—modestly, of course.

Part 2

Birders Described and Illustrated

Early Birder *Podilymbus aurora*

62"–74" (155–188 cm)

Breeding adult wears casual clothing without cargo pockets. No vest. First-winter birder lacks personal binoculars; shares with spouse. Early Birders leave field trips with headaches from trading binoculars back and forth fast, forcing eyes to adjust to binoculars not set—after five minutes—to anyone's eyes.

Endearing curiosity. Early Birder's awed breathing when seeing first bird through spotting scope reinspires jaded birders.

Asked to identify a bird, Early Birder hides by sinking into group or pretending not to hear. Frantic scrabbling through field guide is common; arguing with artist *in absentia* is rarer.

Focuses more on birds than Birder Chic. Questioning aloud correlates with confidence.

Voice: *WHERE is it?*

Range: Population expanding rapidly throughout North America.

Habitat: Backyards, vacation sites, local Audubon field trips.

Worldwide Fulmar *Fulmarus terrarum*

63"–69" (158–175 cm)

Birder who retires young, to bird the world. Color changes with T-shirts bought to celebrate each good Life Bird.

Rapid airport scrambles alternate with stiff-winged glides to meet expert guides in bird-rich locales. Distinguished from Solitary Albatross by light-weight optics, sun-proof clothing, hat with chinstrap. All clothes wash in sink, hang dry in two hours, layer for comfort below freezing.

Pair can live two months out of small wheeled suitcase. Tote optics in padded carry-on.

Worldwide Fulmars have more money than children will ever earn; worry about it. Expanding range. Flock beneath migrating birds.

Home bird feeders stored in garage.

Voice: *When we get home from the Rio Grande, after Costa Rica, we have twelve hours to catch the plane to Point Pelee, before Attu. No time for laundry. It's okay—we bought two sets of clothes. We'll just empty the suitcase and reload.*

Range: Attu to Costa Rica.

Habitat: Tropical, desert, mountain, tundra, island, and pelagic tours; ABA conferences.

Blue-shoed Booby *Sula erratosa*

72"–75" (183–191 cm)

Tall birder with bright blue shoes, loose-jointed gait, graying hair. Friendly. Attains adult size, coloration, and clothing while retaining juvenile interests and judgment.

Chucks small boulders into stream other birders are crossing on a log. Blue-shoed Booby is surprised—then mortified—when muddy water spatters birders on the log. Contritely tries to wipe mud stains from new jackets and favorite trousers. Other birders see in his blush that this happens to him often—and don't mention that he's weakened the stream bank, muddied the stream, changed the streambed, killed a fish, and scared away all birds within shrieking range of the soaked birders.

Voice: *Omigosh! I'm so sorry! I didn't think—*

Range: Irregular wanderer in late summer and fall to inland birding groups, occasionally to Pacific Coast.

Habitat: Birds in flocks that don't know him yet.

Great Gracious Heron *Ardea suaviloquens*

76"–78" (193–198 cm)

Lean gray birder with long legs and neck; may stand over six feet tall. Like other herons, modest about often spectacular achievements.

Deeply passionate about politics of homeland, outspoken on current government figures. Suave in English, but rises to paroxysms of charm when speaking French.

Delightful sense of humor.

Voice: Leaning forward with half-closed eyes: *En français, c'est impossible de ne soit pas charmant dans la présence d'une femme intelligente et jolie. Séduire: c'est la raison d'être de la langue française.*

Range: Europe to North America.

Habitat: Marshes, swamps, tide flats, birding groups with lovely female birders.

Queen Eider *Somateria regina*

63"–66" (160–167 cm)

Take-charge birder with distinctive profile, regal bearing. Has seen every bird species breeding in North America; clear, clean records prove it. Breaks Life List into Continent Lists. Annual Yard List monitors bird numbers in her region. (103 species. Songbirds down dramatically. Birds that used to migrate through in double-digit groups are flying in singly.)

Having achieved her personal birding goals, Queen Eider now focuses on helping her grandchildren discover birds. The royal theory is **We save birds to save ourselves:**

- Birds are visible and appealing; humans rally to rescue birds' nesting and feeding grounds.
- By preserving land for bird habitat, we protect a patch of land in its natural, complex state with all components intact and functioning . . . which then cleanses local air and water—a dialysis machine for humans living nearby.

Voice: *We could learn from birds. When there's no food, they don't raise young. When there's no rain, they don't nest.*

Range: Broadly, but selectively, migratory.

Habitat: Nests in wooded hillsides, ranges widely in search of birds.

Family Mergansers *Mergus familiellus*

64"–74" (163–188 cm)

Fit, slim birders. Mom has red hair; all wear sunscreen. Merganser young spot and identify birds at cyberspeed. Bedtime reading graduates from field guides to ornithology texts.

Mergansers bird apart from organized groups when necessary for young to find birds that excite *them*. Fathers are encouraging, affectionate. Both parents carry their very young on their backs.

The hope of the hemisphere.

Merganser goals: Have fun; know you're bright and good.

Voice: *Yes, that* is *a Ladder-backed! He* is *gouging out a nest hole. I don't know. Let's watch to see if they both work on it.*

Range: Range widely—but not densely enough.

Habitat: Fresh-aired sites with dramatic birds, wholesome birders.

Car Plovers *Charadrius sedentus*

62"–65" (158–165 cm)

Soft people in city clothes and thin-soled shoes. Nonbirding humans who ride with or drive birders to birding sites, but never leave automobile. Own no binoculars or bird books. Never look up from reading material.

Mysterious foraging and sanitation habits. Silent.

Religious Phase: Read Bibles or magazines with pastel illustrations.

Journalistic Phase: Read *New York Times*, even in Western states.

Voice: No sound. (May be incapable of vocalization.)

Range: Not known. More information needed.

Habitat: Parking lots and roadsides.

Loner Yellowlegs *Tringa separata*
and Silent Sandpiper *Calidris tacita*

68"–71" (173–180 cm) and 64"–66" (160–165 cm)

Infertile pair; share female's nest. Fly together to birding activities; dress alike and share food. Mutual needs, fondness for one another, and enjoyment of birding keep them loosely paired.

Yellowlegs works in computers; vast database, from birds to sea lions. Flees fiscal responsibility.

Sandpiper is competent birder with peculiar habit of walking in Yellowlegs's shadow. Sees Yellowlegs's unsuitability . . . against bare horizon.

Voices: *Oh, look. A Yellow-throated Warbler. You don't often see those west of the 100th meridian. Must be a vagrant.*

Nods.

Range: Alaska to Mexico.

Habitat: Marshes, mud flats, shores, pond edges; in summer, open boreal woods.

Napoleon's Gull *Larus bonaparti*

68"–70" (173–179 cm)

Best organized field trip leader. Personally disciplined, demands same of all on his bus. Military background. Good boots. Great legs.

All routes preplanned; no vacillating at Ys on trail. Buses timed to four-minute windows, water jugs full, cups for everyone. Barks crisp instructions; everyone listens. Wife walks last on trail, herding dawdlers to bus on time.

Walks fast, talks fast, finds birds.

Voice: *Here's how we'll do it . . .*

Range: Only worthwhile birding spots.

Habitat: Trails.

Medical Tern *Sterna medica*

68"–72" (173–183 cm)

Graceful, compact birder who doesn't mention his job. No vanity license plates advertise his specialty. Confirming field marks: cell phone in pocket, Jaguar driven on washboard road.

Approaches birding as he did medical school—systematically, to get good. Buys best optics immediately. As beginner, memorizes field marks of target birds for each trip.

Enjoys being with people whose vital signs he's not responsible for. Ironically, attracts flocks of patients by avoiding Me Doctor behaviors.

Doubt arises only when Medical Tern describes a bird as being on "the fourth branch from the base" and you realize it's actually on fifth branch because there's a twig the Tern didn't see.

Voice: A quiet, low *Here. Want to see this in the scope?*

Range: Breeds locally, wanders widely.

Habitat: Large lakes, coastal waters, beaches, bays.

Underemployed Razorbill *Alca furiosa*

66" (167 cm)

Chunky birder, small-eyed and thick-necked; intensely displeased with career. Rarely displays hope for professional fulfillment—alternates disgust at government bureaucracy and rage at corporate refusal to support research and development that would solve this nation's problems.

Articulate and fact-packed, Razorbill provides current, behind-the-scenes insights into courts, chemical crime-detection, patenting, modern laboratory science, and each Trial of the Century.

Restores perspective of anyone slightly bored at work.

Voice: Sharp, explosive *Ridiculous!* Followed by, *If they would only take the long view . . .*

Range: Large cities with sophisticated scientific support for court systems. Migrates widely to follow food sources.

Habitat: Nests on rocky cliffs. Circles alone at sea.

Gregarious Eagle *Aquila amica*

73"–75" (185–191 cm)

Brown hair (sun-bleached), year-round tan. Horn-rimmed sunglasses. *Needs* to be followed. Knows birds; wants to know birders.

Often leads with arms uplifted, keeping his group clustered near, to see the birds he finds for them. Ignores major birds found on his territory by others. Gives clear directions to each site. Counts birders often; extremely well-organized.

Plans cozy restaurant dinners after expeditions; sits at head of table and glows.

Eats anything.

Voice: Booming *Okay! Gather 'round, and we'll* . . .

Range: Uncommon to rare in the east; has moved west.

Habitat: Inhabits mountainous or hilly terrain. Nests in beach condos or mountain cabins.

Big Birder *Haliaeetus felix*

72"–75" (183–191 cm)

Adult readily identified from book jacket photos and television specials. Thick hair. Walks awkwardly on carpeting; sure-footed in boots on soil. Charm is polished organic.

Clear persona—Birdier Than Thou—is marrow-deep, supported by each personal choice: clothing, work, house, car, research topics, and mate. If not wearing sport coat, gives speeches in shirts that match eye color. Lean jeans. Mate is photographer or editor.

Many fly with him, but *Haliaeetus felix* soars—dedication and focus enhancing his natural gifts. Big Birder begins young, grows confident with publication. Full adult plumage is binoculars, spotting scope, camera, and four-wheel-drive vehicle given by manufacturers.

To differentiate Big Birder from other eagles, see who's keynote speaker.

Voice: PssshhwsssshhhwsssshhhhWSSSSSHHHH!

Range: Cape May, Attu, High Island.

Habitat: Bird preserves with solid grants and well-plumbed on-site cabin.

Thin-skinned Hawk _Accipiter membrana_

_66"–68" (167–173 cm)_

Baggy pants treated with Deet, and tank top revealing severe sun damage, distinguish Thin-skin from other accipiters. Female is quick and aggressive.

Hyperalert to patronizing statements by males of any species, Thin-skin interprets neutral remarks as female bashing and goes on offensive. Polarizes groups of birders so that, regardless of season:

- males of all species sprout breeding plumage and give territorial calls.
- females of all species—seeing years of diplomacy and accomplishment threatened—attack Thin-skin, driving her from group or into Gentler Phase.

Alarm call is loud screech. Mating call is plaintive whistle. A woodland hawk, the Thin-skin perches, then dives to attack.

Voice: _Watchit, buster!_

Range: North American mixed woodlands.

Habitat: Tall snags.

Competitive Falcon *Falco competitor*

68"–70" (173–179 cm)

Slaty head with wide black sideburns. Short, powerful stride moves him swiftly to each goal. Competitive Falcon wears custom-made holders for binoculars, guidebook, water, trail mix, and Life List. He designs holders, has tailor make them out of space-age materials. Sweatshirt or jacket matches trousers. Fresh haircuts keep wind-resistance low.

Competitive Falcon birds with groups, but just out of sight, ahead. *Will* see each bird on field trip bulletin; *always* reports rare sightings to group. If birds are gone, sights a mountain lion. Anyone tripping on his spotting scope is told its price.

Voice: *Just 300 yards farther than the group went, we saw a nesting pair of the . . .* (birds the group drove forty miles to see).

Range: Nearly worldwide.

Habitat: Open country, mountains, beaches, groups.

Steadfast Quail *Callipepla fida*

62"–64" (158–163 cm)

Shy birder with distinctive hairstyle, accompanying mate on their first ABA field trip—led by a dynamic ornithologist. Group includes a biology professor, zoo veterinarian, wildlife photographer, and bird-guide illustrator.

For ten years, Steadfast Quail has birded only with beloved spouse of thirty-seven years. She uses Charles's old binoculars since he bought new ones. Wears his khaki windbreaker when he wears his navy one. Charles's bird guide is their resource. He's nearly memorized it, making himself the final authority—*Is it a Herring Gull or a Western Gull? Well, look at the legs and eyes!!*

As identifications flash and surge—quicker eyes and nimbler minds finding familiar birds with new names—disillusion clouds Quail's binoculars. Charles is barely Intermediate!

After lunch, pain subsides when Charles finds a Red Phalarope in a group of Red-necked Phalaropes—and the professor focuses her scope on it while the illustrator photographs it for his files.

Cradling Charles's old binoculars, Quail discovers she can identify Willets before they fly . . . by their unique matte gray legs.

Voice: *So our Royal Terns are really Elegant Terns?*

Range: Wherever monogamy flourishes.

Habitat: Cities and towns, beaches, parks, and resorts.

Duhrect Dove *Zenaida obliviosa*

62"–65" (158–165 cm)

Sweet-faced, slow-blinking. Distinctive walk. Efficient birder: To find a bird quickly with binoculars, stands in front of spotting scope to aim where it's focused. Or walks up *close* to the bird. Obscenities screamed by colleagues often flush birds before Duhrect Dove can see them.

Saves time setting up scope in group field trips by carrying scope with legs extended full-length and spread to three of the four winds.

Good team player: If anyone in the group wonders aloud how many eggs are in a nest, Duhrect Dove pulls the branch down and counts.

Voice: Soft *Ooooh, soorry*—or silence, pretending no one's yelling. Jacket produces fluttering whistle when Duhrect Dove walks fast.

Range: Usually birds alone. Noticed only in group field trips.

Habitat: Right in front of you.

Greatest Roadrunner *Geococcyx maximus*

72"–75" (183–191 cm)

Lean, suntanned birder with shaggy crest and long legs.

Gruff outdoorsman with portable microphone snapped to lapel, laser pointer in right hand, slide-advancer in left. Audubon Club Speaker.

The slides onscreen show Greatest Roadrunner— sunburned, smiling, crest flattened by wind, binoculars held at chin level by gale—in prime habitat: wind-scoured granite.

Also at home in auditorium. Bounds in one step from floor to stage—ignoring stairs, even in dark. Famous museums support travel and research; speeches let him share adventures that amaze and delight him.

Single. Mates briefly; does not participate in raising young. Strong, capable well into old age.

Voice: *Ah, ah, ah, ah* until warmed up.

Range: Worldwide, especially extremes of altitude and temperature.

Habitat: Mountains, deserts, tundra, jungles, podiums.

Great Helpful Owl *Bubo adiutor*

71"–73" (180–185 cm)

Generous size and white sideburns distinguish this birder from others carrying scopes and cameras. A birder since youth; extremely knowledgeable. Secure ego.

Fledgling birders instinctively stand close to Great Helpful to ask, "Is that an eagle?" when it might be a turkey vulture. Or when hoped-for Savannah Sparrow may be a finch. Known throughout range for answering questions softly.

Offered food by grateful new birders.

Voice: A discreet *Mmmm, turkey vulture. Come see his red head in the scope.*

Range: Across North America.

Habitat: Forests to city to open desert.

Theorying Owl *Athene cogitatio*

65"–67" (165–170 cm)

Long legs and intense stare distinguish this cheerful burrower into bird behaviors and physiology. The Theorying Owl *sifts* field trips, with all five senses and an agile mind, searching for significant similarities and striking differences. Discovering a relationship between food choice and feather color brings color to her own cheeks.

Keeps Leonardo-style notebooks.

Carries magnifying glass as well as binoculars. Doesn't *count* birds, *scrutinizes* them.

Voice: *Have you ever noticed that . . . ?*

Range: An owl of open country; at home on golf courses, road cuts, airports—wherever ideas might strike.

Habitat: Nests with easygoing spouse.

Tomboy Swift *Chaetura libera*

64" (163 cm)

Visible in airports near ABA conventions and tour destinations. Cargo-pocketed shorts, sunproof shirt, big boots with fat socks, Tilley hat. Hair is ultra short, long and braided, hyper-curly, or under hat. Long strides, big smile. Makeup is sunscreen plus insect repellent.

Field mark: no purse. Fanny pack and cargo pockets keep hands free and eliminate Purse-strap Shoulder and Briefcase Elbow.

On field trips: leaps off tour bus, swoops along trails, pushes self to personal records on rough terrain, seeks new outdoor sensations.

Revels in asexual clothing, gear, gait, activities, jargon, and information. Wears boots to dinner in hotel restaurant, even when husband dresses up.

Between migrations, *Chaetura* is well-coiffed professional, wearing suit, hose, heels, briefcase, purse, laptop.

Voice: *Is this fun or what?*

Range: Expanding across North America.

Habitat: Nests near work.

Ruby-lipped Hummingbird *Archilochus caelestis*

60"–62" (152–158 cm)

Charming flirt, spicing her life and yours. Lets you know she enjoys your company.

Independent adventuress, certain what she wants. Men lie awake nights scheming to get it for her. Her delicacy and coloring that changes with the light cloak her decisiveness. Southern background.

Tiny, but all parts work. Looks decade younger than her age. Wears only flattering colors and lines. Prefers rubies and emeralds to diamonds.

Her tininess makes others nervous that she travels alone, but quickness and focus keep her safer than big, slow birders. As fearless as good sense allows.

Good scope, excellent binoculars. Budgets time to learn bird facts.

Call is a *buzz* of excitement.

Voice: *Why that would be* lovely!

Range: Across North America, and private adventure tours.

Habitat: Acapulco, Cozumel, Costa Rica.

Paradoxical Woodpecker *Melanerpes contrarius*

62"–64" (158–163 cm)

Streaked birder yearning for mate. Expresses loneliness to other birders, who invite her to carpool and share lunch . . . so she drives alone and eats lunch in her car.

Paradoxical Woodpecker believes American society is "too isolating—raising independence to an art form—" . . . so she lives in Southern California, the transient half of the rootless state. Nauseated by arrogant wealth . . . she works in a Ferrari agency.

Paradoxical Woodpecker has no health insurance, worries about future: Will she afford a home? Can she keep this car running long enough to save for a new one? Is retirement a fantasy? To calm herself . . . she smokes a cigarette.

Voice: A spirited *My goal is . . .*

Range: Migrates worldwide; does not nest.

Habitat: Wherever she doesn't want to be.

Future Kingbird *Tyrannus futurus*

69"–72" (175–183 cm)

Tall, dark-haired adolescent birder. Hawk-eyed, trogon-eared. Brain saturated with avian facts and personal observation. Future Kingbird finds and identifies birds in dense thickets before senior birders can lift binoculars to their eyebrows.

Attends every local Audubon field trip. Finds good birds first, tells those near him, who tell others, until locations are relayed to leader, who strolls over to tell Kingbird, "We have a Lazuli Bunting. Did you see it?" Future Kingbird answers, "Yes"—without mentioning that he found it for the group.

Polite, gracious, modest, with wry sense of humor and surprisingly mature sense of self. Future Kingbird gives reason to believe birds will survive this century.

Voice: *Oh, here's our Le Conte's thrasher.*

Range: Continental U.S.

Habitat: Woodlands, grasslands, clearings, often seen near water.

Frugal Phoebe *Sayornis parsimonia*

62" (155 cm)

Quiet, upright birder claiming to bird because it's cheap—but she could stay home for free. Passionate attachment to favorite bird species and intense preparation for field trips suggest deeper-than-economic commitment to avian activities.

Packs brown bag lunch for field trips, camps on overnights, carefully maintains and protects binoculars and field guide. Wears same boots and birding clothes each week, with shoulder-length hair requiring infrequent cuts. Weathered Evian bottle stuffed in pants pocket for water, homemade trail mix, no Tilley gear.

However, she feeds backyard birds black sunflower seeds and suet cakes, flies to remote islands to bird, and computes Life List by continents. Smiles when says knowledge is more important than spotting scope.

As careful to stay on trails and avoid trampling nesting areas as she is to protect her binoculars from scratches, Frugal Phoebe may regard whole earth as own backyard.

Voice: Soft but determined *No, thanks. This is fine.*

Range: North America and Asia.

Habitat: Coastal villages, desert campgrounds, museums, mountain trails.

Opinionated Jay *Cyanocitta opinionata*

62"–64" (158–163 cm)

Sturdily built birder seeming larger and more common than she actually is. Stakes out high ground when spotting scopes are set up. As new birders arrive at scopes, Jay announces in loud rasping voice each bird they've missed. When Star Birders identify important bird, Opinionated Jay repeats identification clearly and distinctly, pointing when appropriate. Excellent aid for blind birders.

Walking to new sites, Opinionated Jay reviews films, plays, and books, preventing other birders' wasting time and money on weak theatrical productions and inferior literature. Also explains which countries are best to live in, and how to negotiate contracts and run businesses. Gregarious. Optic nerve runs through beak.

Voice: Hearty, nasal—*Sandhill Cranes on the wing. Just above the horizon*, with enormous carrying capacity.

Range: Bicoastal.

Habitat: Oak and pine woods, wetlands, expensive international birding tours.

Host Wren *Campylorhynchus hostus*

70"–73" (179–185 cm)

Energetic, outgoing birder who buys remote real estate, then builds feeders and baths to attract birds so birders flock in. Shows shiny-shoed economists the financial rewards of biosensible refuges nurturing migrants with and without feathers.

Dark brown hair, white eyebrows.

Does own work. Uses all natural materials; structures blend into habitat. Creates bird-viewing areas near his lodge or cabins. Likes large, hand-crafted wooden benches with plaques memorializing birders who spent pleasant hours observing hummers, titmice, and grosbeaks drawn to feeders and baths.

Where three feeders suffice, Host Wren builds eight; his faucets drizzle to invite sippers. He plants uncreosoted telephone poles so woodpeckers drill nest holes for themselves and owls, filling Host Wren's cabins with woodpecker-watchers and owlers.

Voice: *You're in 3-B—overlooking the new Magnificent Hummingbird nest.*

Range: Undeveloped lands convertible into prime habitat.

Habitat: Deserts, mountains where land prices are low—until he establishes his territory.

Saturday Morning Kinglet
Regulus satrapa saturdiurnalia

70"–72" (179–183 cm)

Ideal Field Trip Leader: windfall birder attracting flock of varied species. Apparently egoless, fits niche perfectly. From welcoming a beginner's discovery of a Black Phoebe to deferring to field ornithologists that the hawk posing for the scope is an immature Cooper's Hawk—not a Sharpie—the Kinglet helps each subject feel clever.

Master of meticulously planned field trips that feel spontaneous, the Saturday-morning Kinglet remains in control by never *controlling*.

Keeps track of all his birders, leaving no stragglers to parch in desert. Carries Audubon Club scope and focuses it for new birders. Kinglet sells local bird guides (laminated or plain, folded or placemat-style) to raise funds for Audubon chapter. Spends weekdays scouting sites so he can march his subjects into a canyon and—with eyes closed—name the birds in every tree.

Cherishes subjects' loyalty. To see this kind birder display ferocity, mention rival leader's beginning a Saturday morning group. Share post–field trip lunch with Kinglet to observe whimsy beneath golden crown.

Voice: *Ohhhh, good spotting!*

Range: Best-attended bird groups in North America.

Habitat: Where birders seek empowering leadership.

Audubon's Solitaire *Myadestes auduboni*

70"–72" (179–183 cm)

Slim, graying birder wearing gray pants and windbreaker. Note buff elbow patches, white socks, and running shoes. Silver-rimmed glasses.

Audubon's Solitaire attends Saturday morning Audubon field trips—at radius of forty yards. Carrying only binoculars—having memorized field guide—*Myadestes auduboni* walks ahead, behind, or on bushy slopes overlooking group. Always on time. May or may not sign roster.

Though knowledgeable and cordial when spoken to, Audubon's Solitaire seeks refuge in fifty-yard radius if joined by other birders in the forty-yard orbit.

Voice: Whispers pleasantly to anyone—oddly—near, *There's a Dusky Flycatcher. On the lower branch.*

Range: Highly migratory. Audubon field trips across U.S.

Habitat: Forest to wetlands—off the trail.

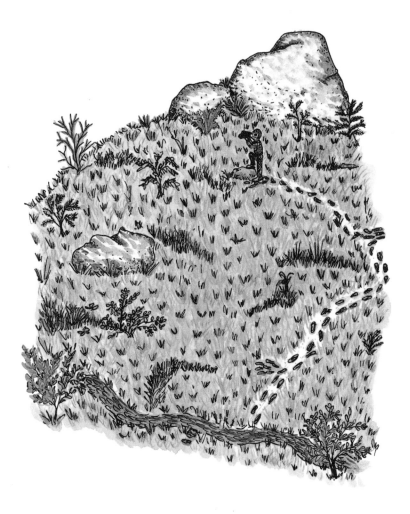

Laser-tongued Shrikes *Lanius acerbus*

65"–68" (165–173 cm)

Shrill pair; impale each other on verbal thorns. No topic too trivial.

Stable symbiotic relationship: each needs victim to attack, to reduce stress of being bullied by spouse. Female is excellent birder; husband attends field trips to be near his beloved.

Aware of personal crabbiness, they laugh at it—then argue.

Often isolated on trail, by birders dashing ahead or lingering behind.

Voice: Exasperated *Well, if you're too hot, take off your jacket!*

Range: Scattered across North America.

Habitat: Thorny brush, fields with barbed-wire fences.

Essential Mockingbird *Mimus necessitas*

70"–72" (179–183 cm)

Identifies birds by songs and calls, focusing group search on correct foliage. Opens apparently meaningful dialogues with birds. Crucial birder for any serious group.

Naturally gifted, self-trained from childhood. Proud to own no birdsong tapes or CDs. Imitates bird calls at parties, meetings, as well as field trips. No credentials; credibility based on accuracy—confirmed when calling birds fly into view.

Center of any expedition for warblers, vireos, gnatcatchers, or grosbeaks.

Voice: *Hear that? Blue-gray Gnatcatcher. Female. Two years old.*

Range: Most effective near home birding grounds.

Habitat: Dense forests and heavy undergrowth.

Bavarian Waxwing *Bombycilla elegans*

64"–66" (163–167 cm)

Diminutive, elegant birder embodying quiet competence. Delightful partner on the trail, his modesty belying a life of adventure and courage only imagined by most. Handles binoculars with a self-assurance honed on multiple continents.

A clue to this birder's fascinating past is his accent shading grammatically pure English. Volunteers no information, but answers each question with political insights indicating current contact with Old Country. Altricial: fine classical education distilled in turbulent century. Adults develop confidence to disagree politely.

Voice: Anything you ask him to say, in Polish, German, or Russian. Responds politely, but less fluently, in French and Italian.

Range: From Europe to U.S., Canada, Argentina, Australia.

Habitat: Open conifers or mixed woodlands, literate birding groups.

Scope-weaseling Warbler *Dendroica turnivora*

61"–63" (155–160 cm)

Unctuously polite birder pretending not to *see* fourteen people lined up behind spotting scope.

Timing, positioning, and speed are key: As one birder steps back from scope to let next person in line have a look, Scope-weaseling Warbler steps in swiftly from the side—in front of birder releasing control of scope—thus in front of next birder in line. Faux-timid "Excuse me," plus smile and head-duck complete the maneuver.

Birders—nonviolent and fair-minded to a fault—give in to parasitism in a state of shock that matures into rage only after Scope-weaseler watches rare bird fly away.

Voice: *I'll just take a peek.*

Range: Found chiefly on edges of groups, facing inward.

Habitat: Gentle birding groups; migrates often.

Paintable Bunting *Passerina pictura*

72"–75" (183–191 cm)

Handsomest North American songbirder. Male: thick wavy hair, well cut; straight white teeth; large direct eyes; dimples; and puzzling smile. Long strong legs and lean torso.

Summer: crisp cotton shirt and khaki shorts with Vasque hiking boots. Winter: Solid color flannel shirt with khakis or jeans.

Disruptive to birding groups of all gender combinations.

Captures prey by smiling at it with both dimples, to paralyze it.

Voice: Cheerful whistling.

Range: All too rare.

Habitat: If we knew, we'd be there.

Well-married Towhees *Pipilo connubialis*

64"–66" (163–167 cm) and 72"–75" (180–188 cm)

Clad in complementary brown suede hats and jackets, their every gesture choreographed by the gods, Towhees love field trips.

Robust and cheerful. Towhees master that sublime balance between independence and loyalty. Each carries personal binoculars, water bottle, trail mix; they alternate toting field guide, note pad, pen. Crossing streams on rocks, or canyons on narrow trestles, Towhee extends a steadying hand as Towshee reaches—knowing hand will be there. In the desert, each brings extra water to share, and keeps track of mate. Both call out, "Car coming" on not-quite-abandoned roads.

Well-married Towhees are mischievous; private security system allows them to *play* in a dangerous world. Symbiotic relationship may even enhance digestion of trail mix.

Voices: *Sweetie! Here's your Vermilion Flycatcher!*
Thanks. Omigosh—a pair of 'em!

Range: Resident from tundra to tropics, in lucky clusters.

Habitat: Field trips, homes, and gardens.

Mystical Meadowlark *Sturnella mystica*

64"–67" (163–170 cm)

Beautiful birder with exuberant song. Streaky hair, squash-blossom necklace.

Eschewing Lists of any kind, Mystical Meadowlark links to birds as individuals. Because birds respond candidly to humans, she is moved to tears of joy when towhees trust her enough to bathe beside her.

Mystical Meadowlark values intimacy with birds—sharing food and garden, providing water, shooing cats, finding nests and telling no one. Watching birds raise young responsibly enhances her confidence in life.

Mystical Meadowlark doesn't mind being scorned by field ornithologists; she knows exactly what they're missing.

Voice: Four *babies? Let me freshen this birdbath for you.*

Range: Canada to Brazil.

Habitat: Her own yard and other secret spots where birds congregate.

Mouse Finch *Carpodacus timidus*

63" (160 cm)

Subtle brown and gray coloring punctuated by alert black eyes. Deceptively knowledgeable, Mouse Finch is universally ignored by leaders.

In gentle voice, solves each vexing mystery on local birding expeditions:

- Why are bulldozers in this bird sanctuary?
- Where is the Canada Goose (minima) that imprinted on a flock of coots and chose to live as a tall coot?

But her explanations soak into mist, unheard by any group leader. Even if repeated by other birders, Mouse Finch vocalizations do not register on leading ears.

Difficult to identify because of camouflage, shy habits, soft voice. Never mates, but owns own nest and five others.

Voice: Exquisitely delicate *These bulldozers are lowering the mean elevation to a gradient sea-level to-sea-level-plus-two-feet, so tidal flushing and natural marsh grasses will restore this bay-dredging dumpsite to a self-sustaining wetlands.*

Elicit this intricate song up to three times by bellowing, "What's HAPPENING here?!?" and pretending to hear nothing.

Range: British Columbia to Southern Mexico, flying and feeding with other common finches, the anonymous observers and defenders of avian rights.

Habitat: Where the birds are.

Soirée Grosbeak *Coccothraustes socialis*

70"–75" (179–191 cm)

Stocky, friendly, easygoing. Dark hair, substantial nose. Gifted joke teller. Relaxing guy. Life is going well for him, so he bears no grudges or irrational hatreds.

Smiles when you drive up. Laughs at your jokes, too.

Good birder, but the reason you invite him to carpool is that his political, economic, social justice, and ecological philosophies match yours. The take-home birder.

Voice: *Okay. Three friends—an Emperor Penguin, an Ostrich, and a Short-tailed Albatross—decide to circumnavigate the globe together. Their travel agent says . . .*

Range: Welcome everywhere.

Habitat: Frequents productive birding sites and good restaurants.

Part 3

Support for the Serious Birder-watcher

Getting Serious

When the moment comes, we know it. We misidentify a birder in front of an expert who says nothing . . . doesn't deign to correct. Or we're asked by beginners, yet again, for assistance we cannot provide.

The time has come to consolidate the scraps of paper into a computerized Life List, and transfer it to rows of checks on a holy parchment from the American Birder-watching Society. The time has come to memorize the birder guide, take classes in birdering-by-ear, and buy original art from a principal birder artist. This will be The Year We Fledge Our Life List.

Part III provides support for the birder-watcher moving to new levels of expertise and fulfillment.

Birder-watching Equipment

In sports and the arts, equipping oneself is a major joy of participation. Birder-watching, too, offers material satisfactions.

Like our prey, birder-watchers *need* only **binoculars** and a **field guide**—which become intimate possessions. We adjust our right ocular to our very own eye so we can flash to a birder and identify, instead of twiddling knobs and adjusting width while the birder ambles off. We share our **binoculars** no more often than our toothbrush.

Our **birder guide** expresses our personality:

- Do we write the place and date we see each new birder?

- Do we write beside the drawing—or the description?

- Do we count only birders we identify personally—or do we rely on the field psychologists in our group?

- Do we bend our field guide's cover back?

- Turn down page corners?

- Affix color-coded plastic tags?

- Carry it with us—or memorize it at home?

As we upgrade essentials and add **secondary gear** like hats, pockets, and spotting scopes, we define ourselves as **Ultimate Opticians** or **Traditionalists**.

ULTIMATE OPTICIANS vault into new millennia. Prosperous and matter-of-fact, UOs see the goal of birder-watching as seeing birders. And if birders are best seen through the newest, clearest spotting scopes, it's only logical to buy the Leica Televid APO, with the zoom lens, Bogen tripod with the microfluid head, and the case. And while the wallet's out, to just go ahead and buy the Swarovski EL binoculars and keep the old binox in the car trunk.

Some Ultimate Opticians say, "I have bad eyes, so I need optics." But, without glasses, they identify birders still in their Jeeps. UOs see that life is short, and equipment enhances it.

Ultimates may have a Big Year after birder-watching only five years. They wear T-shirts from the world's major birder-watching preserves, or 112 enamel pins of birders on their hats. They birder to succeed at birder-watching. Never block a trail they're striding down.

A subset of Ultimate Opticians is comprised of the **Formerly Thrifty**, who have experienced a mind-clearing near-tragedy. These converts buy the brightest, lightest scope on the market, to celebrate having eyes to see through it and arms and legs to carry it.

TRADITIONALISTS, by contrast, realize that birder-watching is far more than a quadruple-digit Life List and being on a first-name basis with the Rare Birder Alert operator. Traditionalists' binocular enamel is worn through to silver metal where their thumbs rest. Trads keep their first field guide with every notation, having it rebound after they nearly lose SANDPIPERS & PHALAROPES in a windstorm.

Trads wear their Favorite Boots, Good-luck Birder-watching Hat, gloves they inherited from Audubon's nephew. They birder-watch in the same places until birders greet them by name. Trads are horrified by newcomers' adding a birder to their Life List without spending quiet personal time observing him.

Some Trads connect to their birders in ecospirituality: We all ultimately drink the same water, eat each other as food. Other Trads have been birder-watching so long that their answer to "Why?" is "I always have." Trads mourn the loss of old names for birders, resist the reclassification of perfectly good species. They enjoy using Ultimate Opticians' great new spotting scopes, but would never buy one.

Traditionalist smugness baffles Ultimate Opticians: If my birder-watching gloves are older than yours, the birders are really *mine*. Trads must be dragged into each millennium by the boots, fingernails clawing new trails through years with too many zeros. But familiar birders will comfort them. Trads will be there—in their Favorite Boots—when it's time to restore habitat for endangered birders. No Johnnies-Come-Lately, they won't be Johnnies-Leave-Early.

The success of hybrids and morphs validates experimenting . . . buying the Newest Best or cherishing what Feels Right—or buying something new and cherishing it. We do express ourselves in our equipment, and we all see birders.

American Birder-watching Society (ABS) Code of Ethics

1. Birder-watchers do not endanger birders, birds, other fauna, or habitat.

- Tape-recorded birdsongs stress birders by luring them away from birds. The ethical birder-watcher uses this powerful tool with care.

- Pishing draws birders who think it's a birder near target birds or—from the lips of champions—a bird. Pishing should be practiced in moderation. (In any case, it works only once per group.)

- Parking in sanctuary roadside pullouts and waiting for birders to pull in is perfectly legitimate.

- Parking, then focusing a spotting scope to decoy birders in, is acceptable if birds are present. But a scope trained on birdless boulders inspires moral considerations. Of course, good birders decoyed in may *find* birds.

- Focusing scopes and cameras on mountain cafés, offering free coffee and decals at Audubon outings, or setting up booths at ABA conventions is as ethical as setting out bird feeders. But birders on breaks are just people. The thrill is seeing them find a bird, argue over field marks, defend their identification in multiple texts, prove themselves correct, then smother their pride in modesty.

(Note: Birder-watchers in Big Years must resort to count-and-run technique. But others needn't sacrifice the joy of observation, the warm chuckling at birdery ways.)

- Birder-watchers do not harass birders carrying juveniles.

- Birder-watchers stay on trails and roads, and never litter. Each maintains habitat for all.

2. Birder-watchers are exemplary persons.

- Birder-watchers take turns at spotting scopes and don't block other birder-watchers' binoculars.

- Birder-watchers do not—too often—burst into conversations, forge ahead of the group leader, talk loudly, or flush birders others want to see.

- Birder-watchers wear khaki, and natural fibers in forest colors.

▪ Birder-watchers speak softly, pronounce birder names correctly, and maintain the endangered lie/lay, who/whom, I/me, affect/effect distinctions.

▪ Birder-watchers do, however, eat trail mix and drink water without sharing.

American Birder-watching Society Decal

To avoid adding plastic to habitat, we ask ABS members to cut out this decal and wedge it against their car's rear window.

American Birder-watching Society's Rules for Counting Birders

To standardize Big Years and Life Lists, the ABS has established the following criteria for counting birders:

1. Each birder must be human. No cats or birds of prey watching songbirds may be counted.

2. Each birder must be observing birds without intent to shoot, trap, pluck feathers, or steal eggs.

3. Each birder must be seen in the field, watching wild birds; i.e., humans watching birds in zoos or cages are ineligible.

4. Each birder must be alive at the time of the sighting. Stuffed or sculpted birders in museum dioramas are not legitimate.

5. Photographs, paintings, films, or videos of birders do not count.

6. Actors portraying birders are not birders.

7. Ordinary curious people looking at a bird don't count, even if they point.

8. Tourists with binoculars and/or cameras must be verified. Birders from foreign countries or out-of-state are prized vagrants—but nonbirding tourists have no place on honest Lists. Visitors must come to the sighting locale to *bird*.

9. In deep thickets, *voices* of birders actively identifying birds are, of course, counted. Birders lunching, napping, or chatting are not.

In all sightings of rare birders, corroboration by a recognized birder-watcher witness is invaluable. Photographs or tape recordings may substantiate lone observations. Physical evidence such as the presence of binoculars in combination with bird guide and/or spotting scope, in the absence of firearms, is circumstantial but significant.

A Birder-watcher's Big Year

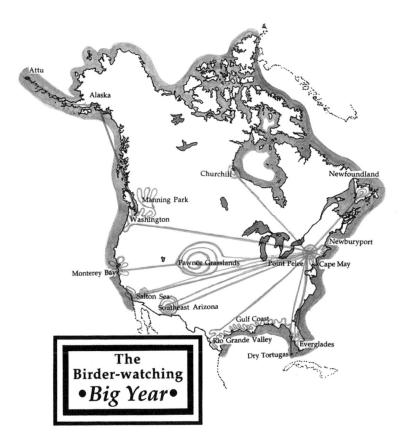

Some birder-watchers with enormous financial support and physical stamina undertake a Big Year, in which they see as many different species of birders (see ABS rules) as they possibly can in one year. Beginning at the first second of a January first, they chase birders until the last second of that year's December. This map shows a typical route.

Prevention of Common Birder-watching Injuries

The most frequent injuries to birder-watchers involve repetitive use of equipment or ignoring ergonomic principles in the use of that equipment.

1. **Binocular Neck:** Stiff neck and shoulders from wearing heavy binoculars suspended around the neck on a narrow strap. (Some believe narrow binocular straps can flatten carotid arteries, inducing fainting and strokes. Unproved.)

Aid A: Buy cushioned strap.

Aid B: Hook cushioned strap over shoulder between birders.

Aid C: Buy harness suspending binoculars from whole upper body.

Aid D: Remortgage house to buy superlight binoculars to attach to harness.

2. **Lactic Acid Arm:** Burning paralysis in forearm, heavy sensation in shoulder—from squeezing binoculars to hold them still when hands tremble after holding binoculars too long on birder who will not step into sunlight.

Aid A: Remortgage for lighter binoculars.

Aid B: Psychotherapy to work through obsessiveness, perfectionism, competitiveness.

Aid C: Professional massage.

3. **Tripod Foot:** Full-body self-loathing and guilt sustained by regretful hyperawareness of foot that stumbled against the Bogen tripod supporting the fragile five-thousand-dollar Questar spotting scope.

Aid A: Wear walking shoes instead of big boots.

Aid B: *Think.* Is it possible these scopers are interweaving trilegs for practical jokes? Or . . . could somebody want a new scope . . . and . . . ?

Aid C: Trip assertively and often until scope-toters avoid you.

4. **Deltoid Death:** Numbness extending from neck to shoulder, from carrying spotting scope on excessively long hikes over brutal terrain.

Aid A: Read description of field trip before leaving home.

Aid B: Marry a surefooted person who doesn't own a scope.

The greatest **health benefit** of birder-watching, beyond obvious fresh air and exercise, is vision improvement. Many bird-watchers' jobs require close focusing—on computer screens, pages of print, columns of figures—and focusing on distant objects rests their eyes. Anecdotal reports describe birder-watchers awakening Sunday mornings, after Saturdays afield, spontaneously reading cartoons without glasses, or experiencing limited front-page success.

Conservation Note

Every birder is precious, no matter how Common. Big Birders attract our awe, but it's Mouse Finches who patrol local governments and Queen Eiders who volunteer in schools. And Theorying Owls who warn us that, like Passenger Pigeons, our own numbers are but temporary refuge.

Ornithologists name species, but it's amateur birders focusing their binoculars on Earth's vital signs who buy sanctuaries. On an interdependent earth, there are no boring birders.

North American Checklist of the American Birder-watching Society

- ☐ Early Birder *Podilymbus aurora*
- ☐ Worldwide Fulmar *Fulmarus terrarum*
- ☐ Blue-shoed Booby *Sula erratosa*
- ☐ Great Gracious Heron *Ardea suaviloquens*
- ☐ Queen Eider *Somateria regina*
- ☐ Family Mergansers *Mergus familiellus*
- ☐ Car Plovers *Charadrius sedentus*
- ☐ Loner Yellowlegs *Tringa separata and* Silent Sandpiper *Calidris tacita*
- ☐ Napoleon's Gull *Larus bonaparti*
- ☐ Medical Tern *Sterna medica*
- ☐ Underemployed Razorbill *Alca furiosa*
- ☐ Gregarious Eagle *Aquila amica*
- ☐ Big Birder *Haliaeetus felix*
- ☐ Thin-skinned Hawk *Accipiter membrana*
- ☐ Competitive Falcon *Falco competitor*

- [ ] Steadfast Quail *Callipepla fida*
- [ ] Duhrect Dove *Zenaida obliviosa*
- [ ] Greatest Roadrunner *Geococcyx maximus*
- [ ] Great Helpful Owl *Bubo adiutor*
- [ ] Theorying Owl *Athene cogitatio*
- [ ] Tomboy Swift *Chaetura libera*
- [ ] Ruby-lipped Hummingbird *Archilochus caelestis*
- [ ] Paradoxical Woodpecker *Melanerpes contrarius*
- [ ] Future Kingbird *Tyrannus futurus*
- [ ] Frugal Phoebe *Sayornis parsimonia*
- [ ] Opinionated Jay *Cyanocitta opinionata*
- [ ] Host Wren *Campylorhynchus hostus*
- [ ] Saturday Morning Kinglet *Regulus satrapa saturdiurnalia*
- [ ] Audubon's Solitaire *Myadestes auduboni*
- [ ] Laser-tongued Shrikes *Lanius acerbus*
- [ ] Essential Mockingbird *Mimus necessitas*
- [ ] Bavarian Waxwing *Bombycilla elegans*
- [ ] Scope-weaseling Warbler *Dendroica turnivora*
- [ ] Paintable Bunting *Passerina pictura*
- [ ] Well-married Towhees *Pipilo connubialis*
- [ ] Mystical Meadowlark *Sturnella mystica*
- [ ] Mouse Finch *Carpodacus timidus*
- [ ] Soirée Grosbeak *Coccothraustes socialis*

Field Notes

Field Notes

Margaret Harmon is the author of *The Man Who Learned to Walk in Shoes That Pinch*, a collection of fables praised as "hedonistic and luxurious" by the *Los Angeles Times*. She has birded on three continents and nine islands, interviewing and observing birders from the internationally famous to local beginners. Her drawings frequently appear in birding periodicals. Margaret lives with her husband in San Diego.